CLASS CLOWN JOKE BOOK

CLASS CLOWN JOKE

BOOK

HarperCollins*Publishers*Ltd

Class Clown Joke Book
Copyright © 2020 by HarperCollins Publishers Ltd.
All rights reserved.

Published by HarperCollins Publishers Ltd

First edition

HarperCollins books may be purchased for educational, business or sales
promotional use through our Special Markets Department.

HarperCollins Publishers Ltd
Bay Adelaide Centre, East Tower
22 Adelaide Street West, 41st Floor
Toronto, Ontario, Canada
M5H 4E3

www.harpercollins.ca

Interior images: Shutterstock

Library and Archives Canada Cataloguing in Publication
Title: Class clown joke book.
Identifiers: Canadiana 20200183370 | ISBN 9781443460583 (softcover)
Subjects: LCSH: Wit and humor, Juvenile. | LCGFT: Humor.
Classification: LCC PN6153 .C53 2020 | DDC j818/.60208—dc23

Printed and bound in the United States of America
LSC/H 9 8 7 6 5 4 3 2 1

CLASS CLOWN JOKE BOOK

What do you call a pig that knows karate?
A pork chop.

What's it like to be kissed by a vampire?
It's a pain in the neck.

Teacher: You have your shoes on the wrong feet!
Ling: *But these are the only feet I have.*

Knock, knock.
Who's there?
Doris.
Doris who?
Doris locked, so will you please let me inside?

Ray: My budgie lays square eggs.

Jay: *Wow! Does it talk as well?*

Ray: Yes, but it says only one word.

Jay: *What's that?*

Ray: Ouch!

What gets bigger the more you take away?

A hole.

A snail is mugged by three turtles. When the police ask the snail to describe what happened, all he can say is, "I don't know, officer. It just happened so fast."

What did the Atlantic Ocean say to the Pacific Ocean?

Nothing. It just waved.

I have a neck but no head. I have two arms but no hands. What am I?

A shirt.

Why couldn't the pony sing?

Because it was a little horse.

Mom: How did you do on your history test?

Greg: *Terribly! But it wasn't my fault. Every question had to do with something that happened before I was born.*

How do you make a St. John's sausage roll?

Kick it down Signal Hill.

What do you say to an alien with three heads?
Goodbye. Goodbye. Goodbye.

"Excuse me," a woman said to the man sitting next to her on the bus. "You have a sausage in your ear." "What did you say?" the man asked. The woman repeated what she had said, only louder: "*You have a sausage in your ear.*" Again, the man asked what she was saying. Finally, the woman shouted: "YOU HAVE A SAUSAGE IN YOUR EAR." "I'm sorry," the man said politely, "but I can't hear you. I have a sausage in my ear."

What's the key to telling a good pizza joke?

It's all in the delivery.

How do you learn about ice cream?

You go to sundae school.

What's got four legs and goes "Boo!"?

A cow with a cold.

What's the best thing about Switzerland?

Well, the flag is a big plus.

Why did the fugitives escape to Canada?

Because they had nowhere else Toronto.

Man to his friend: My dog is so smart, he can talk.

Friend: *Really? I don't believe you.*

Man to dog: Fido, what's the opposite of smooth?

Fido: *Ruff!*

Friend: Big deal. Ask him something else.

Man: *Okay, Fido. What's at the top of a house?*

Fido: Ruff!

Friend: *That's so silly. Your dog can't talk at all.*

Fido to man (later that day): Should I have said "attic"?

GROANER ALERT!

Helvetica and Times New Roman walk into a restaurant. The waiter says, "We don't serve your type."

One bird can't make a pun, but toucan.

People kept telling me to stop imitating a flamingo. Finally, I just had to put my foot down.

Of all cakes, the best is chocolate cake, and the worst is stomach ache.

Knock, knock.

Who's there?

I have a question. Will you remember me tomorrow?

Yes.

Will you remember me next week?

Yes.

Will you remember me next month?

Yes.

Knock, knock.

Who's there?

How could you forget me already?

Cathy: Yum! The muffins are so nice and warm.

Deb: *They should be. The cat's been sitting on them all morning.*

Why do hummingbirds hum?

Because they don't know the words.

How do you make a frog float?

First you put it in a tall glass. Then you add some root beer and ice cream.

Knock, knock.

Who's there?

Howl.

Howl who?

12

Howl you dress for the costume party?

Teacher: Emily, could you please pay a little attention?

Emily: *I'm paying as little as I can.*

Did you hear the joke about the butter?

I'll tell you, but don't spread it around.

What's a cat's favourite colour?

Purrrple.

How do you catch a school of fish?

With bookworms.

Why didn't the skeleton go to the prom?

Because he had no body to dance with.

What happened to the person who stole a calendar?

She got 12 months.

Knock, knock.

Who's there?

Waiter.

Waiter who?

Waiter minute or two while I get ready.

What do you give a sick pig?

Oinkment.

The Fathers of Confederation couldn't come up with a name for their new country, so they decided to place all the letters of the alphabet into a drawer and work with the first three they picked. When John A. Macdonald pulled out the first letter, he said, "*C,* eh?" After picking the second letter, he said, "*N,* eh?" And after the last letter, he declared, "*D,* eh?" And that's how Canada got its name.

Polly: Our teacher talks to herself. Does yours?

Molly: *Yes, but she doesn't realize it. She thinks we're listening.*

Simone: My dog can do arithmetic.

Nina: *Really?*

Simone: Yep! Ask him what 10 minus 10 is, and I'll bet he says nothing.

What's a dinosaur's favourite province?
BC.

Knock, knock.

Who's there?

Jester.

Jester who?

Jester minute—I'm on the phone.

How much dirt can you remove from a hole that's one metre wide and one metre deep?
None. If it's a hole, the dirt has already been removed.

GROANER ALERT!

I took a picture of a wheat field today. It came out pretty grainy.

Albert Einstein developed a theory about space . . . and about time, too!

My mom is getting a fridge for her birthday. I can't wait to see her face light up when she opens it.

I started out with nothing, and I still have most of it.

What animals like bowling?

Alley cats.

"Dad," Sally said to her father, "are bugs good to eat?" "That's disgusting, Sally," her father said. "You shouldn't talk about things like that at the dinner table." After dinner, Sally's father said, "Now, what did you want to ask me?" "Oh, nothing," Sally answered. "There was a bug in your soup. But now it's gone."

What marks do Canadian students get on their tests?

Ehs.

Knock, knock.

Who's there?

Cash.

Cash who?

No, thanks. I prefer walnuts.

Mom: Eat your cauliflower. It's good for growing children.

Kid: *Who wants to grow children?*

Why did the teacher jump into the lake?

Because he wanted to test the water.

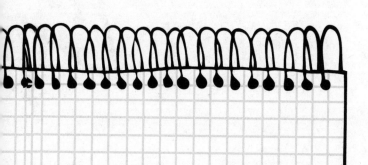

What did the fishin' magician say?

Pick a cod, any cod.

How do killer whales make music together?

In an orcastra.

What happens if you throw a white rock in the Red River?

It gets wet.

Why do we dress babies in pyjamas?

Because they can't dress themselves.

Why is Dr. Frankenstein never lonely?

He is always making new friends.

Do fish ever go on vacation?

No—they are always in school.

What do spies do in the rain?

They go undercover.

What did the mother cow say to the calf?

It is pasture bedtime.

A man phoned an airline office in Toronto. "How long does it take to fly to Halifax?" he asked. "Just a minute," the clerk told him. "Thanks," the man said before hanging up.

Brian: Do you have holes in your underwear?
Ryan: *No.*
Brian: Then how do you get your feet through?

"I hear it's going to rain this morning," the kangaroo says to her friend. "That means the children will have to play indoors all day."

Why are lost things always in the last place you look?

Because after you find them, you stop looking.

What do cows do after school?

They go to the moo-vies.

Knock, knock.

Who's there?

Wooden.

Wooden who?

Wooden it be great if this was the last knock, knock joke?

GROANER ALERT!

It's expensive to train for a marathon, but it's worth it in the long run.

If I had five cents for every bread joke, I'd have a pun per nickel.

I was wondering . . . Why can't hedgehogs just share the hedge?

I can recognize twenty-five letters of the alphabet. I just don't know why.

Madhava: This morning I woke up and felt the dog licking my face.

Sophie: *What's wrong with that?*

Madhava: We don't have a dog.

Teacher: You should have been here at eight o'clock in the morning.

Carter: *Why, did something happen?*

What did the dog say when he sat on a piece of sandpaper?

Ruff! Ruff!

How do hockey players stay cool?

By sitting next to the fans.

Knock, knock.

Who's there?

Ivor.

Ivor who?

Ivor new pair of running shoes.

Why do witches fly on broomsticks?

Because vacuum cleaners are too heavy.

Teacher: If I gave you two goldfish today and three goldfish tomorrow, how many would you have?
Nasir: *Eight. I already have three.*

What's a giraffe's favourite kind of story?
A tall tale.

Knock, knock.
Who's there?
Turnip.
Turnip who?
Turnip the music. I can't hear the song.

What did one snake say to the other snake?
Won't you please give me a hug and a hiss?

"If you had a loonie and you asked your mother for a toonie, how much money would you have?" the teacher asked. "One dollar," answered a little girl in the back row. "You don't know your arithmetic," said the teacher. "No," said the girl. "You don't know my mother."

What do you call a sleeping dinosaur?
A dinosnore.

Knock, knock.

Who's there?

Iguana.

Iguana who?

Iguana new sweater before winter starts.

What did the beaver say to the maple tree?

It's been nice gnawing you.

Why are dogs such terrible dancers?

Because they have two left feet.

Manny: What's pink and blue and eats worms?

Annie: *A pink-and-blue worm-eater.*

Manny: What's red and green and eats worms?

Annie: *A red-and-green worm-eater.*

Manny: Wrong! They only come in pink and blue.

What do cats call mice?
Delicious.

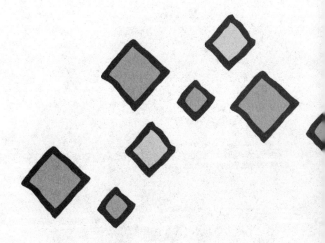

Knock, knock.

Who's there?

Alex.

Alex who?

Alex plain later.
Just let me inside.

Mommy, mommy. Why do I have to go to school today?

Because you're the principal.

What do you call a polar bear in Prince Edward Island?

Lost.

What kind of dog enjoys taking baths?

The shampoodle.

How do you keep a dog from barking in the back seat of a car?

Put him in the front seat.

How do leaves get from place to place?

They use autumn-mobiles.

Why did Dracula ask for a tissue?

He couldn't stop coffin.

Doctor, doctor. My family thinks I'm nuts.

Why is that?

Because I like sour pickles.

There's nothing wrong with that. I like sour pickles, too.

Oh, good. Come and see my collection—I have *thousands* of them!

How do hospital patients make sure they stay online?

They take two tablets.

What do you call the ghost of a chicken?

A poultry-geist.

What's E.T. short for?

Because he's only got little legs.

Why did the sparrow have so much energy?

Because it was sitting on the hydro line.

Three friends are stranded on a desert island. One day, they find a magic lamp. They rub it, and a genie comes out. The genie says that he will give each friend one wish. The first friend says, "I want to go home!" The genie grants the wish. The second friend also says, "I want to go home." The genie grants that wish, too. Then it's the third friend's turn, and he says, "I'm so lonely. I sure wish my friends were back here."

Why did my sister put a tool kit under her pillow?
So she could make her bed in the morning.

Doctor, doctor. I think I need glasses.
You surely do. This is a pet shop.

Teacher: Some months have 30 days and some months have 31 days. How many months have 28 days?
Cathy: *All of them.*

Waiter, waiter. This coffee tastes like dirt!
Well, it was just ground this morning.

What holiday does a vampire celebrate on the second Monday in October?

Fangs-giving.

Teacher: Why are you late for school today?

Andrea: *I overslept because I was dreaming of hockey.*

Teacher: Why would that make you stay in bed?

Andrea: *Because the score was five to five, and the game went into overtime.*

Doctor, doctor. My hair is falling out. Can you give me something to keep it in?

Sure. Here's a paper bag.

How do you divide seven potatoes evenly among four people?

Mash the potatoes.

What's black and white and black and white and green?

Two penguins eating a pickle.

What animal is always at a baseball game?
A bat.

Customer: How much are the chocolate bars?
Clerk: *Two for a dollar fifty.*
Customer: How much is one?
Clerk: *A dollar.*
Customer: Okay, I'll have the other one.

Definition of a snake builder:
A boa constructor.

Knock, knock.

Who's there?

Dewey.

Dewey who?

Dewey really want to
hear any more knock,
knock jokes?

Who's the coolest singer in Canada?

Justin Bie-brrr.

How does the moon cut his hair?

Eclipse it.

Knock, knock.

Who's there?

Anita.

Anita who?

Anita new book to read.

What do you get when you cross a centipede with a parrot?

A walkie-talkie.

Knock, knock.

Who's there?

Abie.

Abie who?

A, B, C, D, E, F, G . . .

Library books we'd like to see:

A Long Walk Home by Misty Bus

Story of the Burglar by Rob N. Banks

Everyone's Favourite Breakfast by Chris P. Bacon

Two Friends on the Beach by Sandy Bums

Going to the Eye Doctor by Seymour Clearly

Swimming in Canadian Lakes by I.C. Waters

Let's All Go Skydiving by Hugo First

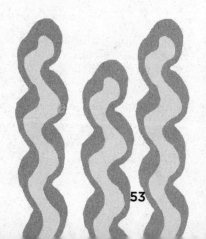

What's a hairdresser's favourite sport?

Curling.

Which side of the tiger has the most stripes?

The outside.

Knock, knock.

Who's there?

Moustache.

Moustache who?

I moustache you a very important question.

Why do lions eat raw meat?

Because they don't know how to cook.

Knock, knock.

Who's there?

Barbara.

Barbara who?

Barbara black sheep, have you any wool?

What can you hold without using your hands?

Your breath.

How much does a pirate pay for corn?

A buccaneer.

What fish tastes best with peanut butter?

Jellyfish.

Why didn't the skeleton cross the road?

Because he didn't have the guts.

Knock, knock.

Who's there?

Lesgo.

Lesgo who?

Lesgo to the cottage this weekend.

What question can you never answer yes to?

Are you asleep yet?

A little boy became ill and was taken to the hospital. It was his first time away from home, and he began to cry. The doctor was concerned and asked the little boy if he was homesick. "No," said the boy. "I'm *here* sick."

Why did the boy stop practising the violin during the holidays?
Because his mother asked for peace on earth.

Why are frogs so good at basketball?
Because they always make jump shots.

What does every birthday end with?
The letter Y.

Two girls were born on the same day, in the same year, to the same mom and dad. They look alike. But they aren't twins. How can that be?
They're two of a set of triplets.

Hailey: Everyone thinks I'm a liar.
Teacher: *I find that very hard to believe.*

GROANER ALERT!

I'm reading a book about anti-gravity. It is impossible to put down!

Turning vegan is a big missed steak.

I decided to sell my old vacuum cleaner. It was only gathering dust.

Nineteen got into a fight with twenty and twenty won.

Knock, knock.

Who's there?

Toad.

Toad who?

Toad you another
knock, knock joke.

Knock, knock.

Who's there?

Olive.

Olive who?

Olive you.

Aw, that's so sweet. Olive you, too.

Sister: Can you skate?

Brother: *I don't know. I've never been able to stand long enough to find out.*

What do we have in December that we don't have in any other month?

The letter D.

Why was the belt arrested?

Because it was holding up a pair of pants.

Teacher: How many seasons are there in a year?

Henry: *Two—hockey and baseball.*

Maya: Ouch! I've been stung by a wasp.

Leah: *You'd better put something on it.*

Maya: I can't. It just flew away.

What animals need oiling?

Mice. Because they squeak.

Why do firefighters slide down a pole in the firehouse?

Because it's too hard to slide up.

What do you get when you cross a bear with a skunk?

Winnie the Pee-yew!

Why did the elephant paint himself in many different colours?

So he could hide in a package of Smarties.

Why was the cell phone wearing glasses?

Because it had lost its contacts.

What's a rabbit's favourite airline?

Hare Canada.

What do you call a musical fish?

A piano tuna.

Knock, knock.

Who's there?

Repeat.

Repeat who?

Okay, I will. Who, who.

What did one elevator say to the other elevator?

I think I'm coming down with something.

Teacher: How many days of the week start with the letter *T*?

Ava: *Four—Tuesday, Thursday, today and tomorrow.*

What did the mama kangaroo say when her baby was lost?

Help! Somebody picked my pocket.

Why was the baseball player arrested after the season?

He stole 50 bases.

Knock, knock.

Who's there?

Not paying attention.

Not paying attention who?

Sorry. Did you say something?

How do you know if an elephant's been in the refrigerator?

There are footprints in the peanut butter.

What happened to the dinosaur after he took the school bus home?

He had to bring it back.

Where do you go to weigh whales?

To the whale weigh station.

Why are barbers such good drivers?

Because they know all the shortcuts.

Why was the baby ant confused at the family picnic?

Because it turned out that all its uncles were ants.

How do you stop strips of bacon from curling in the frying pan?

Take away their brooms.

What goes from *Z* to *A*?

A zebra.

What happens to maple trees every Valentine's Day?

They get sappy.

Why did the ostrich cross the road?

The chicken had the day off.

Mandy: You play Scrabble with your dog? He must be super-smart.

Andy: *Not really. I usually win.*

When does Boxing Day come before Christmas?

In the dictionary.

Why wouldn't the shrimp share its toys?

Because it was a little shellfish.

Knock, knock.

Who's there?

Henrietta.

Henrietta who?

Henrietta big breakfast and doesn't want lunch.

What do pigs do after school?

Hamwork.

What's black and white and slides across the snow?

A zebra on a snowmobile.

What do you get when you cross a parrot with a shark?

I don't know, but when it talks, you'd better listen.

Funny headline: "Crocodiles Go Hungry Due to Shortage of Tourists."

GROANER ALERT!

Ontario's bird got married because it was tired of being aloon.

Buy your soup in bulk at the stock market.

Those insect puns really bug me.

I crossed a homing pigeon with a wood-pecker. It not only delivers a message, but it knocks on the door when it arrives.

Knock, knock.

Who's there?

Norma Lee.

*Norma Lee
who?*

Norma Lee I don't tell
knock, knock jokes.
But for you, I'll make
an exception.

Why don't giraffes need to eat much?

Because a little goes a long way.

Pat: I just bought a parrot for $500.

Matt: *Does it talk?*

Pat: Yeah.

Matt: *So what does it say?*

Pat: "You paid too much. You paid too much."

What's the most musical part of a turkey?
The drumstick.

Robin arrived home after her hockey game.
"How'd you do?" asked her father. "You aren't
going to believe it, Dad," Robin shouted.
"I was responsible for the winning goal."
"That's great," said her father. "How did you
do that?" "I missed my check on the other
team's top scorer."

Why are cooks so mean?

Because they whip cream and beat eggs.

Two fleas were on their way home from
the movies. The first one said to the other,
"Should we walk, or take a dog?"

What's worse than a giraffe with a sore throat?

A centipede with sore feet.

What's worse than a centipede with sore feet?

A walrus with a toothache.

Knock, knock.

Who's there?

Bobby Orr.

Bobby Orr who?

Bobby or Robert—either name is okay with me.

Jenny: Did you know I'm the teacher's pet?

Penny: *Why? Can't she afford a dog?*

Teacher: Can you name four members of the dog family?

Ana: *Sure! Mommy dog, daddy dog and their two puppies.*

Carla: Why are you wearing only one boot?

Marla: *Because I heard there's a 50 percent chance of snow.*

What's smarter than a talking parrot?

A spelling bee.

What do you call a turkey the day after Thanksgiving?

Lucky.

What do you give a sick budgie?

Tweetment.

Knock, knock.

Who's there?

Howard.

Howard who?

Fine, thank you very much. Howard you?

GROANER ALERT!

I cut down a tree just by looking at it. I saw it with my own two eyes.

Two vampires went on a blind date. It was love at first bite.

The mountaineer was disappointed when he reached the highest peak in the Rockies. He knew it was all downhill from there.

PEI's telephone lines are polished by Anne of Clean Cables.

Quiz 1: You may have seen me in Canada's lakes and rivers. Whether I'm going forward or backwards, I'm spelled the same. What am I?
A kayak.

Quiz 2: You may have seen me in a Toronto car race. Whether I'm going forward or backwards, I'm also spelled the same. What am I?
A race car.

Knock, knock.

Who's there?

Lemon.

Lemon who?

Knock, knock.

Who's there?

Lemon.

Lemon who?

Knock, knock.

Who's there?

Lemon.

Lemon who?

Knock, knock.

Who's there?

Orange.

Orange who?

Orange you glad I finally stopped saying *lemon*?

What's the best way to stuff a Thanksgiving turkey?

Give it two slices of pumpkin pie.

What has four wheels and flies?

A garbage truck.

Why do birds fly south in the winter?

It's better than waiting for the bus.

What sound do porcupines make when they kiss?

Ouch!

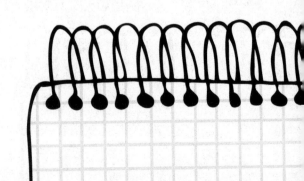

Why did the police arrest the chicken?
They suspected fowl play.

Teacher: If I had three pears in one hand and four pears in the other hand, what would I have?
David: *Big hands!*

What do fireflies say at the start of a race?
Ready. Set. Glow!

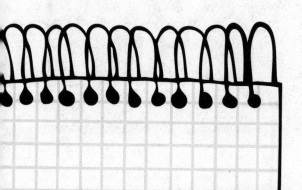

Knock, knock.

Who's there?

Little old lady.

Little old lady who?

That's so cool—
you just yodelled!

How many tickles does it take to make an octopus laugh?

Ten tickles.

Knock, knock.

Who's there?

Juno.

Juno who?

Juno any more knock, knock jokes?

Did you hear the joke about poutine?

It's really cheesy.

Teacher: Alexis, you can't sleep in my class.

Alexis: *I probably could if you whispered.*

Name something that you can put in your right hand but not in your left hand.

Your left elbow.

What did the left eye say to the right eye?

Something between us smells.

98

Doctor, doctor. I think I'm a cow.

Please open your mouth and say moo.

I wondered why the puck kept getting bigger and bigger. And then suddenly, it hit me.

Knock, knock.

Who's there?

Canoe.

Canoe who?

Canoe talk a little louder? It's noisy in here.

Waiter, waiter. How long will my sausages be?

About 10 centimetres, sir.

What do you get when you cross a cat with a parrot?
A carrot.

What do you call an old snowman?
Water.

Why did the cat family move next door to the mouse family?
So they could have the neighbours over for dinner.

What goes zzub, zzub, zzub?
A bee flying backwards.

What did Alex do when her puppy chewed her dictionary?

She took the words right out of its mouth.

What falls in winter but never lands on the ground?

The temperature.

What do cats like for breakfast?

Mice Krispies.

Why should you never steal a mirror?
Because you will feel bad after you reflect on it.

On the first day of school, the kindergarten teacher said to her class, "If anyone has to go to the washroom, please hold up two fingers." A little voice from the back row asked, "How will that help?"

What's a frog's favourite April Fool's prank?
Putting fake sugar in the bug bowl.

Why does marble feel bad?
Because everybody takes it for granite.

Why did the orange go out with a prune?
Because it couldn't find a date.

Why did the student throw her watch out the window?
Because she wanted to see time fly.

Why was the paper bodybuilder pleased?
Somebody told him he was ripped.

Have you heard about the vampire who became a poet?
He went from bat to verse.

Knock, knock.

Who's there?

Police.

Police who?

Police let me
in already.

A man was walking down the street with a penguin. A police officer stopped the man and told him to take the penguin to the zoo. The next day, the officer saw the man again, with the penguin beside him. "I thought I told you to take your penguin to the zoo," the officer said. "I did take him to the zoo," the man replied. "He had such a good time that today we're going to the movies."

What gets wetter the more it dries?
A towel.

Sonia: My dog doesn't have a nose.
Steve: *How does she smell?*
Sonia: Terrible.

Did you hear about the giraffe who got his feet wet?

He caught a cold—two weeks later.

Gina: Ms. Nowak, we ain't got no chalk.

Ms. Nowak: *Gina, it's "I don't have any chalk. You don't have any chalk. They don't have any chalk." Do you understand what I'm trying to say?*

Gina: Yes. So what happened to all the chalk?

GROANER ALERT!

The librarian got off the plane after discovering it was overbooked.

If you eat yeast and shoe polish you will rise and shine!

Nap on the forest floor and you'll sleep like a log.

Farmers make crop circles using a pro-tractor.

After boating through dangerous rapids, I had to pay $5,000 to replace my lost oars, which was a terrible oar deal.

How far can a moose run into the woods?

Only halfway. If it ran any farther, it would be running out of the woods.

Knock, knock.

Who's there?

Beets.

Beets who?

Beets me.

Why do dogs run in circles?

Because it's too hard to run in squares.

What Canadian city is known as "Foot Town"?

Toron-toe.

What has 12 legs and goes slurp, slurp?

A hockey team drinking lemonade.

What's a runner's favourite subject in school?

Jog-raphy.

Doctor, doctor. I feel like a dog.

Sit!

Teacher: There is one good thing I can say about your son.

Mom: *What's that?*

Teacher: With his grades, he can't possibly be cheating.

What's as big as a dinosaur but weighs nothing?

A dinosaur's shadow.

Knock, knock.

Who's there?

Weirdo.

Weirdo who?

Hey! How many weirdos do you know?

Teacher: Tina, did your sister help you with your homework?

Tina: *No! She did it all.*

How many witches does it take to change a light bulb?

Only one. But she changes it into a frog.

Lee: I've lost my dog.

Bea: *Why don't you put an ad in the newspaper?*

Lee: I don't think that would help—my dog can't read.

What do budgies give out on Halloween?
Tweets.

Passenger: Does this train stop in Halifax?
Conductor: *I certainly hope so. Because if it doesn't, you're going to hear a really loud splash.*

Don: My dog is sick, and we're taking her to an animal doctor.
Ron: *Oh! I thought all doctors were people.*

Knock, knock.

Who's there?

Theodore.

Theodore who?

Theodore is stuck. Maybe we can both push it open.

What should you do for an elephant with an upset stomach?

Stay as far away as possible.

What's green and sour and swims in an aquarium?

A trop-pickle fish.

Daughter: Mom, where were you born?

Mom: *Vancouver.*

Daughter: Where was Dad born?

Mom: *Winnipeg.*

Daughter: And where was I born?

Mom: *Toronto.*

Daughter: Cool—isn't it great that we all got together?

The dentist took one look inside Oscar's mouth and said, "That's the biggest cavity I've ever seen. That's the biggest cavity I've ever seen." Oscar looked at the dentist and told him, "I heard you the first time. You don't have to repeat yourself." "I didn't," the dentist said. "There was an echo."

A little boy came home early from school, so his mother asked him why. "Because I was the only one who could answer a question," he told her. "What question was that?" asked the mother. "Who threw the paper airplane at the teacher?"

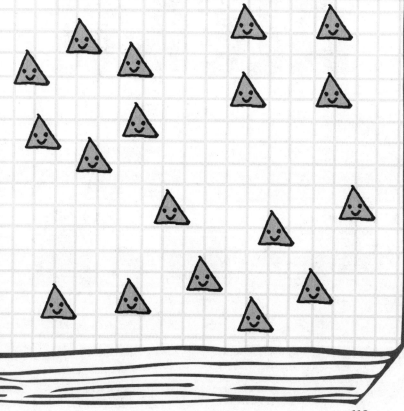

GROANER ALERT!

The Bay of Fundy is strong because it's full of mussels.

To split the Roman Empire, use a pair of Caesars.

My left side went missing—but I'm all right now.

Knock, knock.

Who's there?

Blush.

Blush who?

Why are you blessing
me? I didn't sneeze.

What does Scrooge wear when he plays hockey?

Cheap skates.

A woman walks over to a guard at the museum. "How old do you think these dinosaur bones are?" she asks. "Oh," he replies. "They're three million and three years and two months old." "That's amazing," the woman says. "How can you be so exact?" "Well," the guard answers. "They were three million years old when I started working here, and that was three years and two months ago."

Knock, knock.

Who's there?

Abby.

Abby who?

Abby New Year, everyone!

How can you spell cold with two letters?

IC.

A man went to the doctor and said, "Please help me, doc. I think I'm lucky." The doctor said, "Well, what's wrong with being lucky?" The man said, "Lucky's my cat."

Why was the centipede kicked off the hockey team?
Because he took too long to put his skates on.

Knock, knock.
Who's there?
Boo.
Boo who?
Ahh! Did I say something sad?

A white horse walks into a restaurant. "Do you know there's a city in Yukon named for you?" the waiter asks him. The horse replies, "Bruce?"

Knock, knock.
Who's there?
Icing.
Icing who?
Icing country and western songs. What do you sing?

Coach of winning hockey team: Your players are very good losers.
Other team's coach: *Very good? They're perfect!*

How do you keep a skunk from smelling?

Hold its nose.

Why did Tim Hortons stop baking doughnuts?

Because they were tired of the hole business.

Knock, knock.

Who's there?

The interrupting cow.

The interrupt—

MOOOOO!

What do you call a monkey that wins the Stanley Cup?

A chimpion.

There were two skunk brothers, In and Out. One day, In got lost. The mother skunk sent Out to find him. A little later, both skunks returned. The mother skunk asked Out how he'd found his brother so quickly. "It was easy, Mom," Out told her. "In stinked."

What does a polar bear eat for lunch?
Iceberg lettuce.

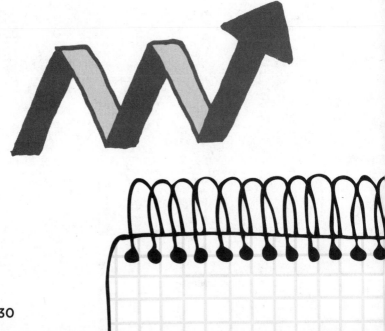

Luis: What's the difference between a mouse and a litre of milk?

Anthony: *I don't know.*

Luis: Well, let's just hope no one sends you to the store to buy milk.

Knock, knock.

Who's there?

Moo.

Moo who?

Are you a cow or an owl?

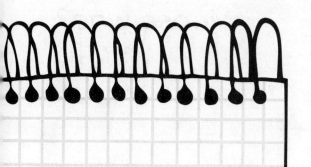

Knock, knock.

Who's there?

Moose.

Moose who?

Moose you keep
telling these
knock, knock jokes?

GROANER ALERT!

I went to the Canary Islands, but I found no canaries. It was the same in the Sandwich Islands. There were no canaries there, either!

I never suspected my dad stole items he found on highway posts, but when I got home, all the signs were there.

If a sheep changes direction, it is a ewe turn.

I asked my grandfather why all his shirts had characters like Frankenstein and Willy Wonka on them. He said he couldn't stop picking up novel tees.

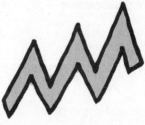

What do caribou have that no other animal has?

Baby caribou.

Knock, knock.

Who's there?

Goat.

Goat who?

Go to the house next door.

What did the softball glove say to the ball?

Catch you later!

What's the difference between a cat and a frog?

A cat has nine lives. A frog croaks every night.

Knock, knock.

Who's there?

Broken pencil.

Broken pencil who?

Oh, forget I asked you. It's pointless.

Teacher: Anna, is it ever correct to say "I is"?

Anna: *"Yes. I is the ninth letter of the alphabet."*

How do you brush a tiger's teeth?

Very carefully.

What happened to the woman who the magician sawed in half?

She's now living in Edmonton and Montreal.

How do you get four ostriches into a minivan?

Two in the front and two in the back.

How do you get a kangaroo into a minivan?

Ask one of the ostriches to leave.

When I take the ferry to Vancouver Island, it makes me cross.

Knock, knock.
Who's there?
Howard.
Howard who?
Howard I know? I haven't even opened the door.

What do you get when you cross a caribou
and a ghost?
A cari-BOO.

A horse walked into a restaurant during the
Calgary Stampede, and the waiter asked him,
"Why the long face?"

Knock, knock.
Who's there?
Woo.
Woo who?
Wow! You're sure excited about something.

Doctor, doctor. I think I'm a kangaroo.
No problem. Just jump up on my couch.

Who lives in Prince Edward Island and bakes funny-coloured bread and rolls?
Anne of Green Bagels.

Knock, knock.

Who's there?

Huron.

Huron who?

142

Huron time today!
That's a surprise!

Teacher: Do you know what "climate" means?

Jordan: *Yes! That's what I do when I see a ladder.*

What's the difference between a mosquito and a fly?

A mosquito can fly, but a fly can't mosquito.

Why did the woman poker player break up with the King of Hearts?

She just didn't want to deal with him anymore.

Why don't scientists trust atoms?

Because they make up everything.

How do grizzlies catch fish?

They use their bear hands.

Customer: I'd like to buy some long underwear.

Clerk: *How long do you want them?*

Customer: Oh . . . from about the beginning of November to the end of March.

What do you find hanging from maple trees?

You find that your arms are sore.

Where do snowmen keep their money?

In snowbanks.

Knock, knock.

Who's there?

Sherwood.

Sherwood who?

Sherwood be happy if you'd let me come inside.

Why is Ottawa the best place to buy a hat?

Because it is the CAP-ital.

Announcement at a railway station: "Will passengers taking the 11:45 train from Montreal to Toronto kindly put it back."

What do cats put in their milk to keep it cold?

Mice cubes.

Knock, knock.

Who's there?

Kent.

Kent who?

Kent you tell from the way I'm knocking?

What hockey team has players who fly over the ice?

The Winnipeg Jets.

Teacher: Fred, what do you call the outside of a tree?

Fred: *I don't know.*

Teacher: Bark, Fred.

Fred: *Okay. Bow wow!*

Knock, knock.

Who's there?

ABC.

ABC who?

ABC who's knocking so hard on the door.

149

What's the best thing to put into a Nanaimo bar?

Your teeth.

Doctor, doctor. I have tulips growing out of my ears.

How did that happen?

Don't have a clue. I planted roses.

Teacher: How old is your dad, Stanley?

Stanley: *He's as old as I am.*

Teacher: How can that be possible?

Stanley: *He became a father the day I was born.*

What hockey player wears the biggest helmet?

The one with the biggest head.

Why don't they play cards in the jungle?

Too many cheetahs.

Teacher: Stefan, I've had to send you to the principal's office every day this week. What do you have to say for yourself?

Stefan: *I'm glad it's Friday!*

Did you hear about the cat that ate a ball of wool?

She had mittens.

Teacher: What's the definition of illegal?

Sasha: *A sick bird.*

How did the basketball court get so wet?

The players dribbled all over it.

Lilly: What animal is grey and has four legs and a trunk?

Willy: *An elephant?*

Lilly: No. A mouse going on holiday.

Knock, knock.

Who's there?

Oscar.

Oscar who?

Oscar silly question, I'll give you a stupid answer.

Teacher: If you add 250 plus 6, divide by 4, and multiply by 14, what do you get?

Jack: *The wrong answer.*

Which is heavier—a kilo of feathers or a kilo of bricks?

Neither. They both weigh the same.

Why did the golfer need a new sock?

Because he got a hole in one.

Gloria: What kind of bug is purple, slimy and smelly?

Sheldon: *I don't know.*

Gloria: Neither do I. But one is crawling up your leg.

Teacher: What's wrong with your eyes, Remy?

Remy: *I keep seeing double.*

Teacher: Stand next to my desk, please.

Remy: *Which one?*

Doctor, doctor. I think I'm invisible.

Next patient, please!

Someone's parents had four sons: North, West and South were three of them. What's the name of the fourth?

Someone.

Waiter, waiter. Your thumb is in my soup.

No problem. It's not very hot.

Did you hear about the twit who took an incredibly long time to drive across Canada?

Whenever he saw a sign that said CLEAN WASHROOM, he did.

What's a ghost's favourite pie?
Boo-berry.

Sam (on the phone): I'm afraid my son can't go to school today.
Principal: *Oh, that's too bad. And to whom am I talking?*
Sam: This is my father speaking.

"Excuse me," the customer said to the butcher, "do you have chicken legs?" "No," the butcher replied. "I always walk like this."

Two hockey players, Raj and Ryan, were talking. Raj said, "I wonder if there's hockey in heaven." A month later, Ryan died. One day, his ghost appeared to Raj and said, "My friend, I have good news and bad news." "What's the good news?" Raj asked. "There *is* hockey in heaven," Ryan told him. "That's great!" Raj said. "Now, what's the bad news?" "Oh," Ryan answered. "You'll be playing goalie on Tuesday."

How can you get four suits for a toonie?

Buy a deck of cards.

What time should you go to the dentist?

At two-thirty.

When do kangaroos celebrate their birthdays?

Only in leap years.

How many letters are there in the alphabet?

Eleven.

How do you make antifreeze?

Take away her blanket.

Why did the cookie go home from school early?

Because it was feeling crummy.

Where do you go to learn to be an astronaut?

To moon-iversity.

What day does a fish hate the most?
Fry-day.

Why did the hockey player bring string to the game?
So she could tie the score.

Why do ant students start the day singing "O Canada"?
Because their teachers like to begin class with the national ant-them.

Knock, knock.

Who's there?

Toronto.

Toronto who?

Toronto the store and
back will take me
about 10 minutes.

What has 88 keys but can't open any doors?

A piano.

Ed: How long were you in the library?

Ted: *About the same length I am now.*

Why was the computer late for school?

Because it had a hard drive.

Doctor, doctor. Will I be able to play hockey after my leg gets better?

Of course.

That's great! I could never play it before.

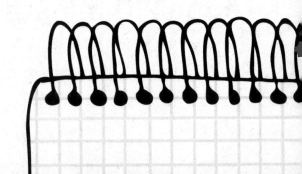

How did they catch the crooks at the pig farm?

Someone squealed.

What did the skeleton drive to the hockey game?

A Zam-bony.

Waiter, waiter. What's this fly doing in my soup?

Looks like the breaststroke, sir.

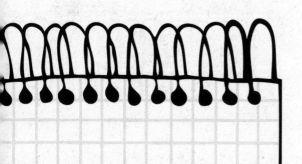

GROANER ALERT!

Don't steal kitchen utensils, unless it's a whisk you're willing to take.

When my giant parrot died it was a real weight off my shoulders.

Two silkworms had a race. It resulted in a tie.

Customer: I'd like some beef, and please make it lean.
Butcher: *Which way?*

What do you eat for breakfast in Canada's capital city?
Ottawaffles.

Why did the lion spit out the clown?
He thought he tasted funny.

Waiter, waiter. Do you serve crabs?

Certainly, sir. Come right inside.

Knock, knock.

Who's there?

Wanda.

Wanda who?

Wanda buy some Girl Guide cookies?

Why *didn't* the rhinoceros cross the road?

It didn't want to be mistaken for a chicken.

Knock, knock.

Who's there?

Surgeon.

Surgeon who?

Surgeon A. Macdonald, Canada's first prime minister.

Why did the man lose his job at the fruit store?

Because he kept throwing the bent bananas away.

Knock, knock.

Who's there?

Wire.

Wire who?

Wire you asking me all these questions?

What do you get when you cross a softball

player with a monster?

A double header.

Knock, knock.

Who's there?

Europe.

Europe who?

No, I'm not! *You're* a poo!

Knock, knock.

Who's there?

Misty.

Misty who?

Misty bus, so now I'm waiting for the next one.

What do you get when you cross an elephant with a reindeer?
Big holes all over the Arctic.

What did the skate say to the helmet?
I think you should go on a head while I continue on foot.

What do you get when you cross a fish with a couple of elephants?

Swimming trunks.

Waiter, waiter. You have your thumb on my hamburger.

I know. I don't want it to fall on the floor again.

Why do dolphins swim in salt water?

Because pepper makes them sneeze.

Knock, knock.

Who's there?

Lettuce.

Lettuce who?

Lettuce in already. We're freezing!

Justin: The dog ate my homework.

Teacher: *Justin, you don't have a dog.*

Justin: It was a stray.

How do you know you're celebrating Halloween in Canada?

You create a costume that will fit over your snowsuit.

What do you call a bear with no teeth?

A gummy bear.

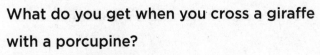

Knock, knock.

Who's there?

Lego.

Lego who?

Lego of my hand, and I'll let you know.

What do you get when you cross a giraffe with a porcupine?

A very tall toothbrush.

What's the coldest month in Canada?

Decembrrr.

Did you hear about the owl with laryngitis?

He doesn't give a hoot.

Knock, knock.

Who's there?

Chester.

Chester who?

Chester moment. I'll be ready soon.

Why did the cow jump up and down on the trampoline?

Because the calves wanted a milkshake.

Knock, knock.

Who's there?

Tamara.

Tamara who?

Tamara is Sunday (or Monday, or Tuesday, or Wednesday, etc.).

Definition of a Canadian:

Someone who knows what a toque is—and maybe even how to spell it.

Why do baby chicks like dollar stores?

Because everything is cheep, cheep!

Knock, knock.

Who's there?

Denise.

Denise who?

Denise and her brother—de nephew.

Where do you find Canada geese?

It depends on where you hide them.

Knock, knock.

Who's there?

Apollo.

Apollo who?

Apollo-gize for not answering sooner.

What do a magician and a hockey player have in common?

They both do hat tricks.

What's the opposite of cock-a-doodle-do?

Cock-a-doodle-don't.

Student A: Can you help me out?

Student B: *Of course. Which way did you come in?*

GROANER ALERT!

I didn't think pigs could fly until the swine flu.

If you go to sleep in a herb garden, you will wake up on thyme.

Morgan caught Charlie giving Alexis hot-house flowers. They found themselves in an orchid situation.

What's the most musical province in Canada?

Mani-tuba.

What's the most musical city in Canada?

Saska-tune.

What did the little candle say to the big candle?

Good night! I'm ready to go out.

Knock, knock.

Who's there?

Freddy.

Freddy who?

Freddy or not, here I come!

What has 18 legs and catches flies?

A softball team.

What is a squirrel's favourite ballet?

The Nutcracker.

What kind of music do wind turbines like?

They're big heavy metal fans.

Why is it that, when you choose groceries, you put them in the cart, but the cashier puts them in the bags?

Because baggers can't be choosers.

Teacher: Julia, please tell the class what water is.

Julia: *It's a colourless liquid that becomes dirty when I put my hands in it.*

If you find yourself on Vancouver Island, covered from head to toe in red paint, what has happened?

You have been marooned.

Why do prefixes get in so many fights?

They are always trying to start something.

Why did the shoppers run to the *Bluenose II*?

They saw that there was a big sail on.

Why couldn't the pirate play Go Fish?

Because he was sitting on the deck.

A man got up every morning to sprinkle pink powder in his front and back yards. One morning, his neighbour asked him, "Why are you always putting powder around your house?" "To keep the dinosaurs away," the man explained. "But there aren't any dinosaurs left," said the neighbour. "Well, then it worked!" said the man.

What hockey player can open any door?
Wayne Gretz-key.

What's the capital of Alberta?
A.

Why did the chewing gum cross the road?

Because it was stuck on the chicken's foot.

Where do hockey players go when they're in New York City?

The Empire Skate Building.

Why did the elastic band go to the baseball game?

It wanted to enjoy the seventh-inning stretch.

Knock, knock.

Who's there?

Dismay.

Dismay who?

Dismay come as a surprise, but your shirt is on backwards.

Why did the twit smell the toonie?

He wanted to know how many scents were in it.

Zack: What's that in the bowl?

Zoe: *It's bean soup.*

Zack: Yes, I can see that. But what is it *now*?

What did the nose say to the finger?

Quit picking on me.

Did you hear about the guy who went to a fight?

A hockey game broke out.

Teacher: Carmen, would you like to name two cities in British Columbia?

Carmen: *I would love to. How about Henry and Judy?*

Why did the little boy go outside with his hands wide open?
Because he heard there would be some change in the weather.

What did one football player say to another football player?
I get a kick out of you.

Knock, knock.

Who's there?

Cargo.

Cargo who?

Nope. Cargo *beep, beep, vroom, vroom.*

What does it mean if you find a horseshoe at the Stampede?

That some poor horse is walking around Calgary in its socks.

Knock, knock.
Who's there?
Itch.
Itch who?
Bless you. Do you need a tissue?

What position does a monster play on a hockey team?
Ghoulie.

Knock, knock.
Who's there?
Spell.
Spell who?
Okay. W-H-O.

A duck walked into a drugstore and bought some lipstick. "Will that be cash or charge?" the clerk asked. "Oh," the duck replied. "Just put it on my bill."

Why was the curler late for the competition?
Because she overswept.

Knock, knock.
Who's there?
Amos.
Amos who?
Amosquito just bit me. Ouch!

Son: Do you like your haircut, Dad?

Father: *It's growing on me.*

What do you get when you cross a dinosaur with a pig?

Jurassic Pork.

Aunt: If you're a good girl, I'll give you a shiny new loonie.

Niece: *Could you make it a dirty old toonie instead?*

Why shouldn't curlers tell jokes on the ice?

Because the ice could crack up.

Knock, knock.
Who's there?
Yukon.
Yukon who?
Yukon come over now. I'm home.

What do you find in the middle of nowhere?
The letter H.

Rosie: Mom, I knocked down the ladder outside.
Mom: *You'd better tell your father.*
Rosie: Oh, he already knows. He's hanging from the roof.

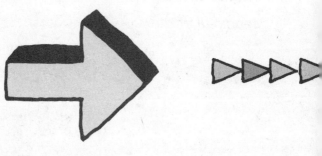

Knock, knock.

Who's there?

Ketchup.

Ketchup who?

Ketchup with me later, and I'll let you know.

What's the difference between an elephant and a chocolate chip cookie?

You can't dunk an elephant into your glass of milk.

Ava: Where are you going on your holidays?

Jean: *Quebec.*

Ava: What part?

Jean: *All of me.*

Where do sheep go for a haircut?

To the baa-baa shop.

Why can't you play hockey with pigs?

They hog the puck.

Knock, knock.

Who's there?

Ducksgo.

Ducksgo who?

No, Ducksgo *quack*. Owls go *who*.

Knock, knock.
Who's there?
Eileen.
Eileen who?
Eileen closer to you so I can hear what you're saying.

Hugh: Have you ever tickled a donkey?
Lou: *No, why?*
Hugh: You'd get a real kick out of it.

Why do soccer players do well in school?
Because they use their heads.

Knock, knock.

Who's there?

Fred.

Fred who?

Fred I forgot my key, so could you let me in?

199

Little league coach: What would you do if it was the bottom of the ninth with two outs, and three runners were on base?
Relief pitcher: *I'd come out of the dugout so I could really see the action.*

Why couldn't the art thief make his van Gogh?
He had no Monet to buy Degas.

Did you hear the story about the tornado?
Spoiler alert: there's a twist at the end.

Why did the hockey player have a light on his helmet?
He was in the miner leagues.

Why did the hockey-playing chicken cross the road?

To get to the puck puck puck.

Principal: Will you pass the mustard?

Teacher: *Only if its grades improve.*

Where do hockey players keep their mayonnaise?

In the dressing room.

What happened when an icicle landed on the hockey player's head?

It knocked him out cold.

Why did the bicycle quit the race?

Because it was two-tired.

Did you hear about the magician from Labrador?

His magic word is "Labracadabrador."

Knock, knock.

Who's there?

Dozen.

Dozen who?

Dozen anybody want to answer this door and let me inside?

What hockey team is always on fire?

The Calgary Flames.

Knock, knock.

Who's there?

Atwood.

Atwood who?

Atwood be nice if you'd finally open the door.

Why did the Timbit go to the dentist?

Because it lost its filling.

What's everybody in the world doing at the same time?

Growing older.

Teacher: Why did you cheat on the test?

Student: *What makes you think I cheated?*

Teacher: Because you had the same answers as the girl you sit next to.

Student: *How do you know she wasn't copying from me?*

Teacher: Well, you and she had the same answers on the first nine questions. And on question number 10, you wrote, "I don't know either."

Knock, knock.

Who's there?

Gopher.

Gopher who?

Gopher another goal, team!

What flies around Parliament Hill all day but never goes anywhere?

The Canadian flag.

What would you do if an elephant sat in front of you at a hockey game?

You'd miss most of the game.

Knock, knock.

Who's there?

Harry.

Harry who?

Harry up and open the door! I need to go to the washroom!

What's the best hockey team in the universe?

The All-Stars.

Why did the chicken cross the playground?

To get to the other slide.

Dad: Can I see your report card?

Kid: *I don't have it.*

Dad: Why not?

Kid: *I gave it to my friend.*

Dad: Why'd you do that?

Kid: *She wanted to scare her parents.*

A boy at the hockey game left his seat to buy a cold drink. When he returned, he said to the man sitting at the end of a row, "Did I step on your toe a few minutes ago?" "You certainly did!" said the unhappy man. "Oh, good," the boy said, "then I'm in the right row."

How do you get a squirrel to be your friend?

Climb a tree and act like a nut.

Jean: How do you like going to school?

Dean: *I like it. And I also like coming home.*
It's the in-between part that's the problem.

Why are ghosts such terrible liars?

Because you can see right through them.

Doctor, doctor. Every night my foot falls asleep.

What's wrong with that?

It snores.

Joe: My barber isn't cutting my hair any longer.

Moe: *How come?*

Joe: Because he's cutting it shorter.

What did the Northwest Territories judge ask the defendant?

Where were you on the night of October to April?

Knock, knock.

Who's there?

Annie.

Annie who?

Annie body want to play cards with me?

Definition of a Canadian:

Someone who's worn a parka and shorts on the same day.

Why was the arithmetic book so sad?

Because it had too many problems.

Knock, knock.

Who's there?

Frances.

Frances who?

Frances capital is Paris.

A woman calls the fire department to report a fire in her neighbourhood. The dispatcher asks, "How do we get there?" The woman replies, "Don't you still have those big red fire trucks?"

What do you call a very small Valentine?

A Valen-tiny.

What did the magnet say to the paper clip?

I think you are very attractive.

Knock, knock, knock, knock, knock, knock, knock, knock.

Who's there?

Your friend the octopus.

Knock, knock, knock, knock, knock, knock, knock, knock.

Who's there?

Now it's your other friend, the spider.

Teacher: Roger, please spell loonie.

Roger: *L-O-O-O-N-I-E.*

Teacher: Leave out one of those Os.

Roger: *Which one?*

What do you find in the middle of Ontario?

The letter A.

What do you call skeletons who sleep in?

Lazy bones.

Customer: How much are these Nanaimo bars?

Clerk: *A loonie each.*

Customer: They're three for a toonie across the street.

Clerk: *So buy them across the street.*

Customer: They're out of Nanaimo bars.

Clerk: *When I'm out of Nanaimo bars, mine are also three for a toonie.*

Why is Alberta the smartest province?

Because it has two As and one B.

Waiter, waiter. This food isn't fit for a pig.

I'll take it back, then, and bring you some that is.

What goes up when the rain comes down?

An umbrella.

Knock, knock.

Who's there?

Wooden shoe.

Wooden shoe who?

Wooden shoe like to let me inside already?

Doctor, doctor. My friend thinks he's a Canada goose.

Bring him in, then.

I can't. He's just flown down to Florida for the winter.

After a heavy snowfall covered its vehicles, what did Canada choose as its new national flower?

A white carnation.

What books do skunks read?

Best smellers.

Teacher: Sam, how do you spell Mississauga?

Sam: *Wrong.*

I said I would run through the campsite but my teacher said I should say "ran," because my running is past tents.

My friend was sad because he doesn't know what a homophone is. I patted him on the back and said, "There, their, they're."

The inventor of the door knocker won a no bell prize.

Fixing the tailpipe of my friend's car was exhausting work.

Doctor, doctor. I feel like a deck of cards.

Sit down and I'll deal with you later.

How do skeletons say hello?

Bone-jour.

Knock, knock.

Who's there?

Kanga.

Kanga who?

Nope. It's kanga-roo.

What do you call bears with no ears?

B*s.*

Why do they call it the CN Tower?

Because when you're at the top, you're "CN" a lot.

How do you know when it's time to clean your room?

When you need to use a compass to find your closet.

Knock, knock.

Who's there?

Carmine.

Carmine who?

Carmine side before it starts snowing.

Doctor, doctor. I feel like a goat.

How long have you felt this way?

Since I was a kid.

What does the prime minister of Canada get on his birthday?

A year older.

Knock, knock.

Who's there?

Willy.

Willy who?

Willy make it, or won't he?

What can you find once in the morning, twice in the afternoon, but never in the evening?
The letter O.

Which burns longer—a short candle or a long candle?
Neither. They both burn shorter.

Why do so many wizards live in Canada?
Because they enjoy the cold spells.

New shoelace: Why are you crying, old shoelace? Can't you tie a bow?
Old shoelace: *No, I'm a frayed knot.*

What do you call it when NHL players skip training?

Playing ice hooky.

Why did the hockey fans wait in a rainy field of wheat?

They wanted to see Grain Wetzky.

What do hockey players sing when a skilled player falls through the ice?

Freeze a jolly good fellow.

What happens if you swap players' hockey sticks for cinnamon sticks?

They play spice hockey.

Knock, knock.

Who's there?

Avenue.

Avenue who?

Avenue already heard this knock, knock joke?

Why did the hockey player dress as Spiderman?

To win the Stan Lee Cup.

Definition of a duck:

A chicken on snowshoes.

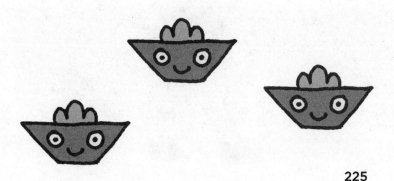

When do monkeys play jokes on their friends?

On Ape-ril Fool's Day.

Knock, knock.

Who's there?

Atch.

Atch who?

Bless you!

Taxi driver: That loonie tip you gave me was an insult.

Passenger: How much do you want?

Taxi driver: Another loonie.

Passenger: Do you want me to insult you twice?

What has antlers and sucks blood?

A moose-quito.

There was a family called the Biggers. There was Mr. Bigger, Mrs. Bigger and their daughter. Who was bigger—Mr. Bigger or his daughter?

The daughter. Because she was a little Bigger.

Knock, knock.

Who's there?

Howie.

Howie who?

Howie doing today?

What did the carpet say to the floor?

I've got you covered.

Mom: How did you do in school today?

Luke: *I got 100 percent.*

Mom: That's terrific. What did you get 100 percent in?

Luke: *Two things. I got 40 percent in geography and 60 percent in arithmetic.*

What's the best season for jumping on a trampoline?

Spring.

Why are false teeth like the stars in the sky?

Because they come out every night.

What did the beach say when the tide came in at the Bay of Fundy?

Long time, no sea.

Knock, knock.

Who's there?

Gladys.

Gladys who?

Gladys you and not someone telling another knock, knock joke.

What's a ghost's favourite lake?

Lake Eerie.

Did you hear about the guy who's afraid of elevators?

He's going to take steps to avoid them.

Knock, knock.

Who's there?

Max.

Max who?

Max no difference. Just open the door!

What do you say to a frog who needs a ride?

Hop in!

What tea do hockey players drink?

Penal-tea.

Trudy: This is a great place for a picnic.

Rudy: *It must be. A million mosquitoes can't be wrong.*

What's Winnie's favourite meal?

Pooh-tine.

What does a cow eat that's made with cheese curds and gravy?

Moo-tine.

Did you hear about the ghost who wanted French fries, cheese curds and gravy?
He walked into a restaurant and asked for boo-tine.

Where do you find the Stanley Cup?
On the Stanley Saucer.

Why did the burglar take a shower before going out to rob the bank?
Because he wanted to make a clean getaway.

Teacher: Are the test questions giving you trouble, Tim?

Tim: *No. The questions are really clear. It's the answers.*

What did the left ear say to the right ear?
Between the two of us, we need a haircut.

What should you do when a pig gets hurt?
Call a hambulance.

Knock, knock.
Who's there?
Shirley.
Shirley who?
Shirley you know who it is—I said I'd be knocking at your door.

How do you get a baby astronaut to sleep?
Rocket.

Teacher: Marco, if you put your hand in one pocket of your pants and found a loonie and a quarter, and put your hand in another pocket of your pants and found a toonie and a dime, what would you have?
Marco: *I'd have somebody else's pants on.*

Knock, knock.

Who's there?

Colin.

Colin who?

Colin all hockey fans. The playoffs are about to start.

Can a kangaroo jump higher than the CN Tower?

Of course. The CN Tower can't jump.

What's a grasshopper's favourite sport?
Cricket.

If Winnie lives in Winnie-peg, where does Otto call home?
Otto-wa.

Knock, knock.
Who's there?
Radio.
Radio who?
Radio not, here I come!

What did the frog say to the teacher who suggested three books for it to read?
Reddit! Reddit! Reddit!

Why shouldn't you wear snowshoes?
Because they'll melt when you go inside.

What is easy to get into but hard to get out of?
Trouble.

Knock, knock.

Who's there?

Tennis.

Tennis who?

Tennis what you get when you add five and five.

What does a duck like to have as a snack?

Milk and quackers.

I think hockey's a great game. Of course, my mother is a dentist.

How do you get a pig to fly?
Buy it an airline ticket.

Knock, knock.
Who's there?
Zany.
Zany who?
Zanybody going to the show today?

Teacher: Chloe, where is your mother going on her business trip?

Chloe: *Saskatchewan.*

Teacher: Very interesting. Can you tell us how it is spelled?

Chloe: *Oh, I just remembered. It's PEI.*

What's a ghost's favourite game?
Hide and shriek.

Knock, knock.

Who's there?

Icy.

Icy who?

242

Duh! You see me.
Do you need glasses?

Knock, knock.
Who's there?
Hugo.
Hugo who?
Hugo first—I'm very polite.

What do pirates eat for dinner?
Fish and ships.

Teacher: Linus, can you tell me what you get when you add four and six?
Linus: *You asked me that yesterday. Did you already forget the answer?*

Knock, knock.
Who's there?
Distress.
Distress who?
Distress is prettier than dat one.

Which hand is it better to write your test with?
Neither. It's best to write with a pen.

What do you call a boomerang that doesn't come back?
A stick.

A polar bear walks into a restaurant and says to the waiter, "I would like a hamburger and . . . . fries." The waiter says, "What's with the long pause?" The polar bear says, "What do you mean? I'm a polar bear."

Knock, knock.
Who's there?
Dishes.
Dishes who?
Dishes your friend (say your name) who's knocking at the door.

If athletes get athlete's foot, what do astronauts get?
Missile-toe.

Where can you find cities, towns, shops and streets, but no people?

On a map.

Julia: What are the three most common words heard in a classroom?

Maria: *I don't know.*

Knock, knock.

Who's there?

Cook.

Cook who?

Hey—are you calling me cuckoo?

Why didn't the orange go to school?

Because it wasn't peeling well.

Knock, knock.

Who's there?

Luke.

Luke who?

Luke out! Here comes another knock, knock joke!

Knock, knock.

Who's there?

Rufus.

Rufus who?

Rufus leaking, and I'm getting drenched.

New student: So what's the worst thing at the school cafeteria?
Old student: *The food.*

Did you hear about the butcher who backed up into the meat slicer?
He got a little behind in his work.

How do frogs say goodbye?
"Have a hoppy day!"

Judge: You look familiar. Have we met before?
Defendant: *Yes—I was your daughter's music teacher. I taught her to play the drums.*
Judge: Life in prison for you!

What letters of the alphabet say goodbye?
CU.

Definition of a Canadian:
Someone who has more kilometres on their snow blower than on their car.

Teacher: Ethan, I hope I didn't just see you copying.

Ethan: *I hope you didn't either!*

What do you call a sleeping bull?
A bulldozer.

Knock, knock.

Who's there?

Pasta.

Pasta who?

Pasta bread and
butter, please.

Did you hear about the man with the musical toilet seat?

Poor guy! Every time he tries to sit down, it plays "O Canada!"

How many seconds are in a year?

Only 12. January second, February second, March second . . .

Why don't bananas snore?

They don't want to wake up the rest of the bunch.

Mother: Are you doing your homework right now?

Son: *I'm doing my homework. Whether it's right is another matter.*

Teacher: If you bought four butter tarts for two dollars, what would each one be?

Hannah: *Stale.*

What did the teddy bear say when it was offered dessert?

No, thank you. I'm stuffed.

GROANER ALERT!

When someone stole my lamps I was de-lighted.

If money doesn't grow on trees, why do banks have branches?

A dinosaur with a large vocabulary is a thesaurus.

German sausage jokes are just the wurst.

A mom texts her son: Hi! What do IDK, LY and TTYL mean?

During his lunch break, the son texts back: I don't know. Love you. Talk to you later.

The mom sends him another text: It's okay, dear. Don't worry about it. I'll ask your sister— and I love you, too.

Knock, knock.
Who's there?
Tank.
Tank who?
You're welcome.

What starts with an *E*, ends with an *E* and has only one letter?
An envelope.

Knock, knock.
Who's there?
Izzy.
Izzy who?
Izzy home yet?

259

Why did the hockey player put glue on his hockey stick?

To make it more hockey sticky.

Why shouldn't you release fierce sharks onto a frozen rink?

You might get frostbite.

Why did the hockey player wear a winter boot on his head?

So nothing would slip his mind.

Why did the hockey player go to the fish shop?

He wanted to buy a pair of skates.

Paul: Should I be punished for something I didn't do?

Teacher: *Of course not.*

Paul: That's good. Because I didn't do my homework.

Doctor, doctor. I think I've lost my memory.

How did that happen?

How did *what* happen?

Teacher: Hello, class. We will have only half a day of school this morning.

Kids: *Hooray!*

Teacher: And we'll have the other half this afternoon.

What do you get when you cross a comedian with a tricycle?

Someone who is wheel funny!

Jeremy: What book are you reading?

Antonio: The History of Glue.

Jeremy: Is it any good?

Antonio: *I can't put it down!*

What day of the week are most twins born on?

Twos-day.

What did the calculator say to the math student?

You can count on me.

Knock, knock.
Who's there?
Pudding.
Pudding who?
Pudding on your shoes before your socks is kind of silly.

Teacher: Dolores, it's the fourth time you're late for school this week. Do you know what that means?
Dolores: *That it's Thursday.*

265

Did you hear about the restaurant on the moon?

The food is great, but there's no atmosphere.

Did you hear about the other restaurant on the moon?

It's out of this world.

Knock, knock.

Who's there?

Philip.

Philip who?

Philip the gas tank before we head to the cottage.

Doctor: Did you take my advice and sleep
with the window open?
Patient: *Yes.*
Doctor: Did you lose your cold?
Patient: *And my wallet.*

Knock, knock.
Who's there?
Adam.
Adam who?
Adam away! I'm coming in!

What's a snake's favourite subject in school?

Hiss-tory.

Pete and Repeat were sitting on a bench.

Pete fell off. Who was left?

Repeat.

Pete and Repeat were sitting on a bench.

Pete fell off. Who was left?

Repeat.

Pete and Repeat . . .

A book fell on the librarian's head.

She has only hershelf to blame.

How many chocolate bars can you eat on an empty stomach?

Only one. After that, your stomach won't be empty.

Why was the baby strawberry crying?

Because his parents were in a jam.

Knock, knock.

Who's there?

Sarah.

Sarah who?

Sarah reason why this door is locked?

Teacher: Class, please open your geography books. Who can tell me where England is?

Logan: *I know! Page 25!*

What has a bottom at the top?

Your legs.

What did the monster eat after he went to the dentist?

The dentist.

Jason: My new computer will do half my schoolwork for me!

Mason: *That's terrific! Maybe you should get a second one.*

Why did the student eat her homework?
Because the teacher said it was a piece of cake.

Knock, knock.
Who's there?
Justin.
Justin who?
Justin time. Dinner is on the table.

Why did the nose join the school track team?
Because it liked to run all day.

What room has no floor, no walls, no doors and no ceiling?

A mushroom.

Doctor, doctor. I have only 50 seconds to live.

Wait a minute, please.

273

Knock, knock.

Who's there?

Mikey.

Mikey who?

Mikey is in my winter coat, so I can't open the door.

What did one potato chip ask another potato chip?

Shall we go for a dip?

How did the snake sign its Valentine's Day card?

Love and hisses.

Knock, knock.

Who's there?

Needle.

Needle who?

Needle little help opening this door?

What's the difference between a teacher and a train?

A teacher says, "Spit out your gum." But a train says, "Choo-choo."

GROANER ALERT!

The reason a hockey arena is so cold is that it has so many fans.

I spotted a lion at the zoo, so now she looks like a leopard.

Don't worry if you see one suitcase frozen in the snow. It's just an ice-olated case.

I asked the janitor why he hadn't cleaned the arena. He said, "I couldn't sweep a rink last night."

Where do astronauts keep their sandwiches?

In their launch boxes.

What would you get if you crossed a bridge with a car?

To the other side.

Dad: How did you do on your first day of school?

Son: *Not too well. I have to go back tomorrow.*

What kind of vehicle does a foot doctor drive?

A toe truck.

Mimi: I wish I'd lived a hundred years ago.

Gigi: *Why?*

Mimi: Because there wouldn't be so much history to learn.

What's the shortest month of the year?

May. It has only three letters.

What do you call two banana skins?

A pair of slippers.

Knock, knock.

Who's there?

Watson.

Watson who?

Watson this afternoon? Are we going skating?

What did the pirate say when he turned 80 years old?

Aye, matey.

What did one tonsil say to the other tonsil?

Let's get dressed up. The doctor is taking us out tonight.

Why are hockey players good at making friends?

Because they know how to break the ice.

What kind of materials do dinosaurs use for the floors of their cottages?

Rep-tiles.

Teacher: Nathan, please name two pronouns.

Nathan: *Who, me?*

Teacher: Excellent, Nathan!

Where did the little ghost go during the day?

To a day-scare centre.

What did one antelope say to another?

So tell me, what's gnu?

Dad: What did you do in school today?

Grace: *We played a guessing game.*

Dad: I thought you had a geography test.

Grace: *Yep! That's right.*

How many sides does a box have?

Two—the inside and the outside.

Knock, knock.

Who's there?

Noah.

Noah who?

Noah good knock, knock joke or two?

285

you can be a
class clown, too.
WRITE YOUR OWN
JOKES here! →

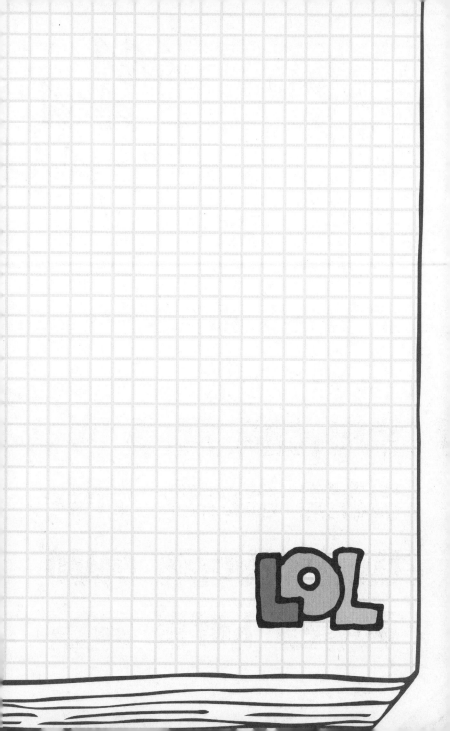

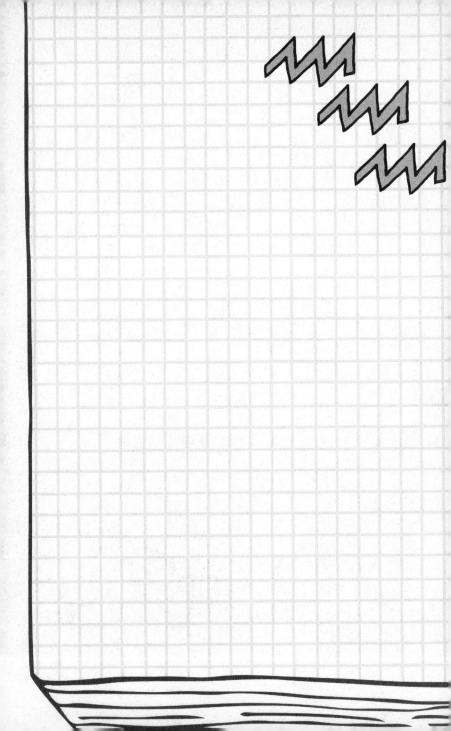